Perfect Wardrobe

Capsule Wardrobe, Curated Closet (Personal Style, Your
Guide, Effortless, French)

Stacy S. Sullivan

D1292592

Perfect Wardrobe: Capsule Wardrobe, Curated Closet (Personal Style, Your Guide, Effortless, French)

Table of Contents

Book 1 - Capsule Wardrobe

Essential Plan For Creating Your Minimalist Wardrobe
(Dream Wardrobe, Mindful Living, Simple Elegance)

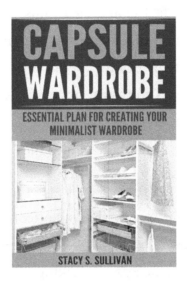

1 - Introduction

In this fast-paced world where no time should be wasted, you can't really spend too much time figuring out what to wear. Due to the fast-changing trends in the clothing industry, it's understandable why a woman would have an overstuffed closet filled with pieces that are trendy today, but not tomorrow. The result, however, is that she stresses over what to wear every day since all she has are statement pieces that aren't interchangeable and are only good for one-time use.

This is one reason why British style icon Susie Faux came up with the capsule wardrobe—to give women style and confidence without necessarily taking up too much of their time getting dressed up. Capsule wardrobe remains popular decades after it was first conceptualized not because it limits the number of clothes a woman has to wear, but also because the limitation in choices allows her to get dressed faster without compromising her personal style.

If the idea of putting together your own dream capsule wardrobe appeals to you, then you've come to the right place. This book contains all the essential information you'll need to start putting up your own capsule wardrobe.

1 - INTRODUCTION

For the next chapter, you'll learn about what a capsule wardrobe is, its benefits, and how Susie Faux came up with the idea.

Another discusses how factors such as your body type, personal style, lifestyle, favorite color palette, and many more can help you decide which clothes to put into your capsule wardrobe.

Next, you'll learn how having a capsule wardrobe can help inspire mindful living. Most people who have built their own capsule wardrobes share that they now have a more heightened sense of consciousness on what they put into their closets. This consciousness helps promote mindfulness, which is particularly helpful when it comes to keeping a capsule wardrobe.

The last chapter shares concrete suggestions on which pieces to put into your capsule wardrobe to keep it simple yet functional.

2 - What Is a Capsule Wardrobe?

A lot of people nowadays continue looking for ways to make use of their time efficiently, and creating a capsule wardrobe is one way. A capsule wardrobe is composed of a finite number of clothes that are often minimalist and are interchangeable. Though the principle behind it is "less is more," the size of a capsule wardrobe depends entirely on what you want. Basically, a capsule wardrobe should consist of high quality clothes that aren't only minimal, but are also clothes that you would love to wear frequently.

A Quick History

Some of us might be hearing the term capsule wardrobe for the first time, but history states that this has been going on since the 70s. While today's capsule wardrobes may have thousands of different varieties to suit different lifestyles, the foundational principle of having interchangeable, minimalist clothes remains basically the same.

The term capsule wardrobe was first coined by British boutique owner Susie Faux, who currently owns a boutique in London called Wardrobe. Growing up surrounded by people who tailor clothes for women, Faux developed a consciousness seeing how well-fitting clothes make a person appear confident and more beautiful.

As a grown up, she started working in the advertising industry, further igniting her passion towards helping other women dress just as well as the males. This led her to open Wardrobe in 1973, waving her battle cry of inspiring women to have confidence and style.

It wasn't until 1980 that the term capsule wardrobe made a debut in Faux's book entitled "Wardrobe: Develop Style and Confidence." Together with a UK-based designer, Jil Sander, she carefully crafted the wardrobe to have a minimalist, foundational aesthetic wherein fewer clothes of higher quality will be included. According to her, a capsule wardrobe creates confidence and success because of the overall look created from high quality pieces.

The book, which was then meant for career women, became like a road map—guiding women to dressing with ease without losing the professional look. For this to be possible, you'll need to have a few core pieces: blouse, coat, bag, belt, dress, jacket, sweater, skirt, trousers, tights, and shoes. While a capsule wardrobe is minimal, there's not standard size of a wardrobe and varies entirely from person to person.

Benefits

The versatility of a capsule wardrobe is not only what makes it popular, but also a few other benefits as well. There are three main benefits of creating your own capsule wardrobe.

First, a capsule wardrobe saves time. Due to the minimal pieces in a capsule wardrobe, getting ready in the morning can be done much faster. Packing for trips can be done in just a few minutes because the pieces you'll bring with you are interchangeable, thus eliminating the need to bring a lot. Also, having few clothes means doing less laundry, so you'll have time to do more important things.

The second benefit of a capsule wardrobe is that it saves energy. A minimal wardrobe reduces the feeling of anxiety and stress from having to choose what to wear every time. In addition, wondering which clothes to pick on a daily basis somehow promotes emotional fatigue. Having only a few choices reduces that fatigue and allows you to spend your energy to focus more on other things.

Lastly, the best benefit you can get from a capsule wardrobe is that it saves you money. Because the pieces in a capsule wardrobe are versatile and can be mixed and matched easily, you won't have to spend as frequently for new clothes. Capsule wardrobes also kick out clothes that can only be worn once, so that's more value for your money there.

In 1985, American designer Donna Karan brought the concept to the United States. She put up her own clothing line—Seven Easy Pieces—which also caters to contemporary career women. The foundational piece of clothing in her line is a black body suit which can be built to a full outfit by adding more pieces.

If you've reached this point and realized that building a capsule wardrobe would be perfect for you, simply head on to the following chapters.

3 - Building Your Dream Capsule Wardrobe

While Faux identifies in her book "Wardrobe: Develop Style and Confidence" some core pieces for a capsule wardrobe, there are no strict rules as to what style and how many pieces you'd like to have. You don't even have to go on a shopping spree to build one. If you're clear on what your fundamentals are and you know exactly what you want, shopping will be made easier and you'll achieve that wardrobe that truly expresses your style, flatters your body, and makes dressing up so much easier for you.

Before you start culling your wardrobe and hitting the stores, here are some tips you'd like to keep in mind when building your dream capsule wardrobe.

Identify Your Body Type

Using a measuring tape, measure your bust, shoulders, hips, and waist. The following are the different body types according to the width of these extremities.

- Heart-shaped – the bust and shoulders are wider than your hips.

- Pear-shaped – the hips are wider than your bust and shoulders.

- Hourglass-shaped – if there's only little difference between the widths of your shoulders and hips.

- Rectangle-shaped – your bust, hips, and shoulders are of the same width (or have very little difference in measurement).

These are the four most common types of body shape. Using these as your reference will help you choose pieces that are flattering and will complement your body.

Find Your Colors

In fashion, it's important to find clothing that'll flatter your skin tone. There are mainly four different skin tones—light cool, dark cool, light warm, and dark warm.

Each of these skin tones has a set of color palettes that are flattering and would greatly serve as a complement. For example, a dark cool skin tone works best with jewel tones (bright colors) while people with light warm skin tones would find pastel colors especially flattering. Try on different colors to see which colors are best for the color of your skin for that confident and polished look.

Defining Your Personal Style

The most crucial part towards building your own capsule wardrobe is knowing what your personal style is. Adopting capsule wardrobe recommendations on Pinterest wouldn't always work if the pieces don't fit your natural, personal style. Narrow down your choices and check which clothes best express who you are. This way, shopping will be less of a hassle and you'll have the confidence to actually wear what you put into your capsule wardrobe.

Consider Your Lifestyle

Capsule wardrobes should suit your lifestyle. Faux mentioned that her book is for career women, which explains why she included trousers, dresses, blouses, and other corporate-looking items as her core pieces.

Consider where you spend most of your time in. Are you an office worker? An on-the-go photographer? Or a gym instructor? Making a list of your daily activities could help you see what your daily life is like, and from there you can narrow down the type of clothes that would suit those activities.

Declutter Your Closet

Scrap out any clothes that you don't use anymore, or those that don't make you feel confident anymore. Note that this'll be extremely challenging, but brutal honesty is a must if you want to rid your closet of all those unwanted clothes to make room for what is truly essential.

After you're done detoxifying your closet, you have the option to donate, store, or throw out your unwanted clothes. Think of this activity as your stepping stone to a fresh, new start, and that you're doing this to make way for pieces that'll only serve to boost your confidence and style.

Create Formulas of Your Dream Outfits

Start thinking about outfit combinations (you can look at Pinterest or Lookbook for inspiration). Building outfit formulas helps make shopping easier, as you already know what pieces you are looking for. Are you a jeans-T-shirt kind of person? Or do you need to have more smart casual pieces? Start your formulas by determining the basic pieces, and pairing them with other items until you achieve your ideal formula.

Go for the Basics

The best, solid foundations for any capsule wardrobe are staple, basic items. You will want to build upon these basic pieces to make great outfits. Think of the basic pieces as the bottom-most part of a pyramid, and the ones on top are the statement pieces. Basic pieces can range anywhere from a white button-up blouse, a pair of black skinny jeans, a beige sleeveless top, and many more.

Include the Shoes

It is important that every capsule wardrobe has a versatile pair of shoes. Ideally, there should be three pairs of shoes that can go with any outfit you can think of in your capsule wardrobe. Do you love masculine shoes such as boots and oxfords? Are you more of a doll shoes type of person or do you prefer heels more? Make sure that the shoes you wear are also comfortable and that the colors go well with your outfits. The safest choices rest with neutral tones such as black, brown, or nude.

4 - Practicing Mindful Living through a Capsule Wardrobe

The journey towards creating your dream capsule wardrobe starts with mindfulness.

Mindfulness is a state where your consciousness is at its peak. You may be wondering what the connection is to creating a wardrobe, but apparently adding and taking out clothes from your closet involves some sort of awareness.

Most people who have created their own capsule wardrobes swear that it helps them become mindful of the clothes they wear, that the clothes aren't just mindlessly bought for the purpose of having something new to wear. Creating a capsule wardrobe doesn't only help you become mindful of the clothes you buy, but also of their quality and purpose.

Here are some tips that can help shift your perspective about the clothes you put in your closet.

Practicing 'Quality over Quantity'

Another principle behind capsule wardrobes is 'less is more.' While you might be thinking why on earth would you have less clothes when the fashion industry is a fast-paced world, a small, minimal closet is actually more functional.

Invest in quality fabrics. The first thing to consider is how the fabric feels in your hand. If the fabric feels nice and drapes well, then it could be a sign that the fabric is of good quality.

Opt for well-made basics. As mentioned previously, basic pieces serve as a solid foundation for all the outfits you will be creating from your capsule wardrobe. Make sure to choose quality, well-fitting basics.

Consider the number of times you can wear a piece. The best technique to creating a functional capsule wardrobe is including pieces you wear in different ways. The more versatile an item is, the more valuable it is to your capsule wardrobe.

Choose the best fit. Don't always pay attention to the size labels since there is no universal sizing chart in the clothing industry. Always buy items that fit you well regardless of the size labels.

Own Your Personal Style

Another mindfulness practice is knowing your personal style, and owning it. This will help you shop for pieces more easily, and will reduce the time and money wasted on clothes that you'll never wear.

Today over tomorrow. Stuffing your closet with clothes, thinking you'd use them in the future is not a mindful practice. Only buy what you are going to be wearing for the present.

Neutrals over loud colors

While it's not a crime to choose clothes with loud colors, keep these choices limited to only a few statement pieces. Choose neutrals as your basics because they're easier to mix and match.

Stick to your style

While there's no harm experimenting, wearing clothes that define your style helps bring out more confidence.

Choose classic, timeless pieces rather than bold, trendy ones

The fashion industry creates trends to inspire more purchases from people. If you stick to basic pieces that will last you years regardless of the trends, you'll be able to maintain a sustainable closet, without the need to buy every time a new trend comes in.

Your Closet Is a Reflection of Your Lifestyle

If you want to keep a mindful closet, it's important that it stays organized. Being conscious of your possessions is nearly impossible if you can't see them all. The first step to an organized closet is decluttering it and taking note of the following.

Display your clothes properly. Nothing defines 'organized closet' as displaying your clothes the way you should. Fold your shirts properly or hang up your coats with care.

Apply the 'one in, one out' principle. If you want to avoid a stuffed closet, take an item out every time you buy new ones. You can either donate it or put it up for sale.

Launder with care. Read the labels on your clothes before throwing them all together in the washing machine. Some fabrics are not meant to go in the washing machine, and doing so will only ruin them. Treat and launder your clothes with care for them to last a lifetime.

Knowing where your clothes are made. While this isn't always followed by all people, some are mindful enough to check out where their clothes are made, particularly whether the workers are treated well by these clothing companies.

While these tips may seem difficult at first, it's pretty easy to maintain a mindful closet once you've started step one. It's advisable to start during the weekend, where you have more free time to become more conscious about your closet. If you can't manage it in one weekend, try adding a bit more consciousness in the next weekends to come and you'll have a more mindful wardrobe in no time.

5 - Basic Pieces to Include in a Simple yet Elegant Capsule Wardrobe

A capsule wardrobe should consist of clothes that will never go out of style. As much as you loved statement pieces before, you should keep these to a minimum if you want to start building your capsule wardrobe. With less options, mostly consisting of basic pieces, you'll be able to plan your outfits more easily. Remember that owning a capsule wardrobe means you'll have clothes that you can wear frequently and interchangeably with the other pieces.

Even though Faux has already shared her core pieces in her book, you are free to tweak it according to your own taste or style. In this chapter, you'll read about a sample capsule wardrobe, and more detailed information on why the basic pieces are essential.

What Should Go Into Your Wardrobe?

The previous sections in this book consisted of basic tips that allow you to adopt the mindset to help you build your own dream capsule wardrobe. This time, you'll read about the staple pieces that serve as the very foundation for building a capsule wardrobe.

Here are the suggested capsule pieces:

- 3 bags

- 2 blouses

- 3 coats

- 2 dresses

- 2 pairs of skinny jeans

- 5 pairs of shoes

- 2 scarves

- 2 skirts

- 2 sweaters

- 2 shirts

- 2 tank tops

- 2 work trousers

Bags (3)

A large, spacious bag is necessary for when you need to carry a lot of stuff with you. This is great for when you plan to go on a trip, to the gym, or when you just need to bring a lot of your stuff with you.

Another bag is one that you can bring with you daily, particularly for work. Choose a simple one in a neutral tone so that it can accompany any type of outfit. Choose one that has both a strap and a handle, so you can carry it any way you want.

Lastly, a clutch bag is great for when you need to go on a night out or to formal events.

Blouses (2)

Include a simple blouse and a statement blouse in your closet. The simple one should be in a neutral shade (white, beige, black, or nude) so that it can be used interchangeably with your jeans, trousers, etc. The statement blouse should create a statement look but can still be worn with flat shoes or jeans during the daytime or with trousers and heels at night.

Coats (3)

The reason why you need three coats is because there are different seasons. For the winter, a heavy coat is the best choice, but note that you should keep this in a muted color.

Another type of coat you can include is a camel trench coat that can be worn over any outfit without warming you too much. If you want to go for that effortless chic look, then this is a great addition.

Lastly, a denim jacket is great to wear during the spring and summer season. It's casual enough to wear with jeans and T-shirt, but can also be thrown over a classic dress at night.

Dresses (2)

It's important to buy a dress that can be worn multiple times for different occasions. A classic dress can be paired with sandals or flats during the day, and can still be paired with heels and a clutch bag in the evening. This can also be worn with tights to make it look professional and sophisticated enough for work.

The second type of dress you should have is a patterned

one. This is useful for events such as nights out, dates, or parties. Make sure to choose a patterned dress that can easily be dressed down or dressed up with the right accessories and footwear.

Skinny Jeans (2)

With skinny jeans, you could never go wrong with the colors indigo and black. These are the only classic colors you'll need when it comes to jeans. They can go with any top, and can be leveled up by simply pairing them with the right shoes and accessories.

Shoes (5)

Shoes are often left-out when it comes to keeping a minimal wardrobe, but you don't need to have that many shoes in your closet. All you need are 5 pairs of shoes which can be worn to just about any occasion.

First, you'll need comfy flats. You can slip your flats on easily for the effortless look. Plus, it can be worn with jeans or with a classic dress.

Next, you'll also need pointed flat shoes. Fashion experts

say that wearing pointed shoes adds a touch of elegance to your outfit without compromising the simplicity of a daily look. Wear it with jeans or trousers during the day, or pair it with a dress for an elegant night out look.

Third, a timeless choice would be black boots. Wear them with jeans for that rock chic look, or with a dress for that Gossip Girl flair.

Next, invest in pointed toe heeled pumps that will be your go-to shoes for a sophisticated look. For a dressed up look, pair them with jeans. Wear them with jeans for a casual yet elegant look.

Lastly, a flat sandal (preferably embellished) is a great must-have for summer. It should be neutral in color so it complements any outfit you wear. The embellishments make it wearable even on a summer night.

Scarves (2)

For the winter, a heavy scarf is a must. A knitted one is the best choice as it's great for keeping you warm. Stick to neutral tones once again to make it suitable to wear with any of your outfits.

Also throw in a light scarf that can be used in spring to block out a bit of sunlight. This should be made from light materials such as satin or silk. It can also double as an accessory; simply tie it around your neck as worn by chic French women.

Skirts (2)

For skirts, you should have one that you can wear during the day and one that can be worn at night. The daytime skirt should be flowing and can be worn with a simple blouse or sweater. For an androgynous, casual look, try wearing it with denim jackets and boots.

Sweaters (3)

First, you'll need a simple, lightweight sweater to wear daily. Note that the style should be simple and that the material isn't too heavy so that you can wear it for all seasons.

Next, a patterned sweater is great for when you want to look bolder and more put together.

Lastly, a knitted lightweight sweater is ideal for layering over s and blouses. You can even bring this with you just in case you find yourself a bit chilly during fall.

Shirts (2)

Probably the most staple piece that'll last you a lifetime are shirts. You can make do with only two of these, one white and one black. These two colors are great with almost any-thing paired with them, and you can dress them up easily with accessories.

Tank Tops (2)

For the summer, you'll need a casual tank top that you can use when the weather's warm. Again, choose a muted color that's comfortable, simple, and can easily be paired with a skirt or a pair of jeans.

The second tank top you should have should be versatile enough to be worn during the evening. For this, choose a dressy tank top, one which you can also wear as a statement piece during the day but can double as a classy, elegant top at night.

Work Trousers (2)

For work trousers, all you need are two colors: black and grey. Grey is the choice color to wear during the months of summer and spring, while black trousers are especially popular during the winter. The great thing about trousers is that they can also make a great evening look when paired with the right heels.

6 - Conclusion

Your wardrobe reflects your personal style, your lifestyle, and how you are as a person. A cluttered, overstuffed closet is most likely a reflection of how disorganized and indecisive you are, especially when it comes to getting ready for the day.

A capsule wardrobe not only limits the number of clothes you own but also helps you become more mindful of what you put into your closet and how you arrange them. As a result, you'll be able to plan your outfits more efficiently, and getting ready in the morning will be faster because you already have your outfit formulas planned beforehand.

Putting together your dream capsule wardrobe may sound intimidating at first. Not only do you have to take out the clothes that don't serve you well anymore, you'll also need to become more discerning of what you buy for your closet in the future. Just take into consideration the tips you've learned in this book and you can easily put together your own dream capsule wardrobe in to time.

Book 2 - Curated Closet

Find Your Personal Style And Create An Amazing Capsule
Wardrobe (Minimizing Your Closet, Step-By-Step)

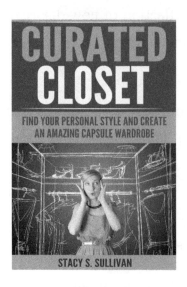

1 - Introduction

One of the most basic needs in life is clothing. But beyond the rudimentary need for protection against external elements, clothes can play a much bigger role. The way you dress is very often an indication of who you are.

The thought immediately goes to uniforms, be it for students or professionals like cops, military or medics. A person in a three-piece suit is going to be perceived in a very different way than someone wearing hoodie and sweatpants. Saying "blue-collar" or "white-collar" is in itself short-hand for different types of labor.

Clothing also has a lot to do with personal expression. Individual fashion choices can signal certain things. Someone who is very feminine can opt for clothes that are pink or with floral patterns. Someone with elegant and refined taste may feel their best and most confident in a suit and tie, while someone else thinks that the best things to wear are a plain T-shirt and denim jeans. As fashion designer and stylist Rachel Zoe puts it, "style is a way to say who you are without having to speak."

This book will teach you how to have a curated closet through defining and refining your personal style. To push that concept further, you can even opt to have a very pared down, minimal look with the help of a capsule wardrobe.

Having a limited choice when it comes to fashion may seem counterintuitive, especially with the way that fashion is often marketed as having everchanging styles and trends. But the beauty of being able to define your personal style is that your look will be distinctive in itself, even if you choose not to hop on to the latest trend. It's also a real powerful move to have a signature look.

With simple steps, you can start the journey towards a curated closet full of clothes that fit your aesthetic and lifestyle. These are the clothes that will make you feel comfortable, beautiful and that you'll want to keep and wear forever.

2 - Reflection

A lot of decluttering challenges on the internet begin with taking all items and dumping them into one place. We'll get to that, too. But before this, you should reflect first and be truly honest about two essential things. First, what do I want to achieve with my capsule wardrobe? Second, what kind of person am I?

The first question targets aspirations and will define what items should be prioritized. The second one gets to the basics and eliminates choices right away very quickly. Let's answer that one first.

Knowing Yourself

Your answer to the question "what kind of person am I?" informs a lot of your decisions when it comes to personal style. Since your style is a form of self-expression, you should make sure that it communicates your identity very well. The answer can be something simple like, "I'm a creative person." It can also be very detailed, such as, "I'm someone with a very formal work environment, but I prefer comfort outside of work."

Your assumptions with regard to your personality will then

eliminate a lot of the clothes you already have. Perhaps you love color and prefer loud, bold hues when it comes to fashion. If so, having some "classic" pieces may not suit you at all regardless of common wisdom, like a white tee, black pants or even the signature little black dress.

It can even extend to areas that are more intangible. Let's say you identify as environmentally and socially conscious. Then you might be compelled to only have items that are locally-sourced, fair trade, second-hand or made with recycled or recyclable fabrics.

Practically speaking, you should also consider the climate of the place where you live. While you may like the thought of walking around in a sleek trench coat, you may be in a hot climate where wearing such a piece would be highly impractical if not impossible.

Conversely, if you live in areas with fluctuating climate, then you will need to consider a rotating capsule wardrobe for the spring/summer and fall/winter that will swap items in and out depending on the need (most likely when it comes to footwear and outerwear).

Another factor about your lifestyle of course has to do with your work. What is your work environment like? Are you required to wear formal clothes? If so, you may want to invest in a suit and patent leather shoes. Or perhaps you're a freelancer who works from home. If so, you may not need any formal pieces like blazers, button-down shirts or tailored trousers.

Finally, think back to your favorite things to wear. What kind of clothes are those? What do you like about them? If given free rein, what would you prefer to wear and why? Your goal when it comes to curating your wardrobe should be to capture as closely as possible the way you feel in your favorite clothes. That's what would make having a minimal closet practical, easy and desirable instead of limiting or diminishing.

Knowing Your Aspirations

Now, let's get to your goals. Why are you interested in a minimal wardrobe? What do you hope to achieve? Your aspirations will define your priorities later on when you have to sort out your clothes.

One of the reasons people cite is practicality. Having a limited number of pieces makes fashion decisions easier. In this case, you need a capsule wardrobe that is highly flexible; where everything can be mixed and matched with everything else. It will be streamlined and cohesive but may force you to be unable to follow trends or pick bolder choices.

Another goal is to make better shopping decisions. You're probably familiar with the feeling of having "nothing to wear" despite a jammed pack closet filled with clothes. If you feel out of control financially, having a minimal wardrobe will force you to invest in quality pieces that you can wear more for longer, and not fast-fashions items that quickly fall out of style or get ruined quickly. As an additional challenge, you can opt to not shop for anything until you wear out that item in your capsule wardrobe.

Perhaps you're starting on a new job and you want to look very adult and refined. Therefore, you would need classic pieces like a crisp white button-down, tailored pants, cashmere jumpers and a camel coat. On the other hand. it could also be that you want to be more stylish and experiment more when it comes to fashion. In that case, you can keep some basics and then pad up with other pieces such as modern or sculptural accessories or bolder outerwear. You can introduce new fabrics or cuts into your closet as well.

Altogether, this step will crystallize in your mind what you want out of your wardrobe. Now, it's time to solidify it and start sorting clothes.

3 - Decluttering

It's highly unlikely that anyone can truly be starting from scratch when it comes to fashion. Of course, you've come to accumulate clothes throughout life. Take everything out of your closet, dressers, and suitcases and place them all in one place.

Now, it's time to get them all and sort them into types: shirts, dresses, pants, coats/outerwear, underwear, sportswear, accessories, jewelry, footwear, etc. Finally, you now get to categorizing, the most basic of which is keep, try, sell/donate and recycle/trash.

Keep

When it comes to this pile, be brutally honest. These are the clothes you are guaranteed to keep and will make up the bulk of your capsule wardrobe. Upon first pass, try and keep a number in mind and stick to it. Let's say, strictly keep 50 items only. You can go through these items a second time with stricter guidelines of preference, lifestyle and goals to further pare it down.

A handy guideline is to ask yourself if you've worn this item in the last 3 months. If not, you probably don't like it anymore and are just holding on for no reason. Inertia will be your enemy if you let it. Be strict, be honest and only keep the essentials.

Try

Undoubtedly, you'll come across some items you aren't entirely certain about. For one thing, perhaps it doesn't even fit you anymore. For these items, put them together in a pile and be sure to try them on and then categorize accordingly. Don't get caught up in trying to fit items in. "These pants will fit me if I lose 5 pounds!" If it doesn't fit, get rid of it.

Your capsule wardrobe is for your real self, living your real life. The same is true for items that are too short or too tight. You want to be comfortable in your clothes. That's not going to happen if you're holding on to pieces of clothing that fit your ideal self rather than who you are right now.

If you're unsure because of factors other than fit, then you can keep a "maybe" pile. If within the next three months you find that you had no need to get anything out of this pile, then discard them from your wardrobe permanently as well.

Sell/Donate

For items that don't make your keep or maybe pile, assess if they're still in good quality. If you're looking to make a quick buck, you can hold a garage sale or sell items online. You can also go to consignment stores and have your clothing appraised there. Otherwise, you can also donate.

In order to maximize clothing donation, make sure you're giving away items that are wanted in the first place. For instance, some charities specialize in giving unemployed people formal clothes to wear for job interviews. Some stock up on coats, boots and blankets to give away during the winter. For novelty items like costumes, you can ask around rental places if they can take it or swap it for something else. You can also donate usually non-reusable clothing like prom dresses or gowns.

Recycle/Trash

Finally, anything you don't want to keep and can't sell or donate should be trashed or recycled where possible. Cotton shirts can first be turned into rags for cleaning. Otherwise, sort items by type and find a place where you can drop off materials for recycling. Most of it will be shredded and turn into stuffing or insulation.

Some are turned into industrial rags. Others are just baled and sold by weight. While very little recycled textile is actually turned into new clothing, at least you'll be thinking about the back-end process of clothes you've bought and will buy in the future.

4 - Defining Your Style

With a pared down closet, you can more easily see which items fall into your personal style. For someone who's employed, for example, you can expect formal or smart items dominating the wardrobe with some casual pieces thrown in for going out during the weekends. Someone with a more expensive lifestyle may have exclusively suits, dress shirts and tailored pants in their wardrobe; casual may mean cashmere jumpers, loafers and cigarette trousers instead of cotton T-shirt and leggings.

Find the Connection

Whatever is left in your closet after your extensive decluttering is guaranteed to be your favorite items; items that suit your preference and lifestyle. While you may not know how to label your personal style yet, now you can easily see the similarities which connect them with ease.

The easiest element to spot is color. Color palettes usually are pretty distinctive of styles by themselves. If your closet is dominated by white, khaki, brown and navy, you're likely to have a more classic, timeless style.

Having mostly black items err on the side of chic and sophisticated, but with some bright and bold colors mixed in black pieces may be the foundations of a more modern, avant-garde style. Earth tones usually dominate the relaxed, Bohemian style while a rainbow of colors fit right into whimsical, more playful and creative styles.

Another style element to be on the lookout for is patterns. Most classic or chic styles tend to favor plain colors over patterns of any kind. If you have patterns at all, it may be on the outerwear only, like houndstooth, pin stripes or plaid. Athletic styles recently favor more graphic patterns or camouflage in a variety of colors, as well as large designer names.

Tartans, gingham, argyle and madras are considered quite preppy and feature in a lot of sophisticated looks. Trendy looks may have animal prints such as tiger and zebra stripes, leopard prints or giraffe spots.

When it comes to item types, you may also find that you're a fan of layering in which case you'll have plenty of basic pieces like tees and tank tops as well as layering pieces like vests, jackets and cardigans or even decorative lingerie, bustier or lace-type items, too. For girls, you may find that you prefer dresses and skirts or, alternatively, pants and shorts only. In which case, you won't be needing any of the other types in your capsule wardrobe since you don't feel comfortable wearing those at all.

In terms of material, natural textiles like cotton, silk, and wool dominate most classic styles. More casual and laidback styles include clothing in cotton, jersey, blue denim and linen. Edgy/subculture styles tend to incorporate a lot of leather, dark and distressed denim and metallic hardware. The bohemian style incorporates a lot of handmade textiles like saris, dyed wool, weavings, and knitwear.

5 - Try on a Label

At this point, based on the choices you made when decluttering and the connections you find in the clothes left in your wardrobe, you may already have in mind what kind of style is your dominant or combination personal style.

Depending on where you look, some of these may go by different (albeit related) names or be combined under one category. Nevertheless, being able to properly label your style will help you going forward in terms of streamlining your style further, branching out to try other styles, or simply be a handy guide when shopping.

Classic/Timeless

A style that has stood the test of time. The classic style tends to incorporate basic and smart pieces that can be dressed up or down. Includes a trench coat, Breton stripe shirt, straight-cut jeans, white button-down shirt, tailored blazer, ballet flats, little black dress and black dress pants.

Vintage

Clothing that harkens back to a time long ago. Usually inspired by fashion from the 20s to the 50s or even up to the 70s. Heavy on lace, floral dresses, silk chiffon blouses, sheer items, cardigans and tights or black stockings. Often styled with vintage necklaces, kitten heel boots and small handbags.

Bohemian

Characterized as "hippie" or "gypsy" looks. Popularized in the 60s and 70s. Emphasis on neutral and earth tones in soft and flowy fabrics. Often feature exotic patterns and textiles in layers. Include maxi dresses, oversized blouses, fringed denim, off-shoulder tops, suede boots, sandals, tunics and furry gilets. Often styled with a head accessory like a headband, bandana or flower crown.

Artsy/Creative/Avant-Garde

Fashion as wearable art. Creative styles tend to dabble in bold colors, mixed prints and patterns and unusual silhouettes. Often cannot be defined by trends as they tend to be ahead of the curve and only subsumed by the mainstream after considerable time. Clothing is often accessories by large, chunky and architectural outerwear, shoes and jewelry.

Casual

Comfort above all else. Characterized as relaxed, laid-back and rugged. Basics include cotton shirts, denim pants, khaki shorts, hoodies, skater skirts, and athletic wear like sweat suits and leggings. Often does not include any jewelry but can be accessorized with a beanie, sun glasses and baseball caps. Footwear could be tennis shoes, sneakers, running shoes or flip flops.

Preppy/Geek Chic

Think school uniform vibes. Characterized as clean, refined and collegiate. Includes blouses and dress shirts, A-line skirts, opaque tights, cardigans, Mary Janes, scarves, headbands, pea and cape coats and thick-rimmed eyeglasses. This style also often includes nautical themes like the Breton stripe, anchor prints/accessories, and loafers.

Chic/Sophisticated

A lot like the classic style, only more high status. Exudes power, wealth and refinement. Designer and luxury brands dominate this look. Most pieces are tailored and custom. Often also monochromatic black and white, with only hints of grey, navy, camel and burgundy as touches of color. Includes custom jewelry, high heels, patent shoes and designer handbags.

Edgy/Rocker

Inspired by subcultures like rock, punk or goth. Casual items are often included but with more graphic statements and heavy use of leather and metal elements. Leather jackets are a must. Black is the most dominant color. Often styled with distressed denim, fishnet stockings, studded belts, jackets and boots, platform shoes and leather pants or skirts.

Trendy

Always up-to-date. Following trends and keeping up with celebrity looks and items inspired by the fashion shows. It may be harder to have this style if you're keeping a capsule wardrobe, but it is still possible if you keep to a couple of basics and have on rotation several accessories instead.

Sexy

Tends to flaunt body shape and feature cleavage, legs, and exposed stomachs. Often tight-fitting, short or low-cut. Includes bodycon dresses, miniskirts, cropped tops, cut-out styles, lingerie, lace and sheer fabrics.

Girly/Feminine

Romantic and sweet. Almost exclusively feature dresses in light or pastel colors. This includes floral designs, frills, ruffles and lace which are often styled with a thin, long cardigan, long necklaces, small handbags, platform heels or ballet flats.

6 - Conclusion

Defining your personal style and curating a minimal capsule wardrobe around it will help you communicate and express your identity, aesthetic and lifestyle clearly and easily. Besides that, it is a practical and frugal way to organize your wardrobe in order to maximize your time and your visual impact. Having a curated closet leads to your signature look; that way of dressing that is distinctive and indicative of your individual personality.

After decluttering your closet, you can focus on paring down what items remain. Try them out and see if there's a particular thing that's missing from your wardrobe. Perhaps you have too many tops but not enough pants or skirts in rotation.

It may be that you don't often find yourself wearing dresses at all. Or it could be that you need less shoes and can take away 3 or 4 more pairs. Perhaps you only have jacket and might need a heavier coat as well. The more time you spend with your clothes, the more you can tailor them to your lifestyle and preferences.

And if you should feel as though your capsule wardrobe has grown predictable or stale, you can always refresh it with new items, or reintroduce items you've kept back. You can keep alternates to basic items like a striped shirt in place of a basic, plain one. If you have a monochromatic look, try picking a certain color to brighten it up.

Deep reds, navy and green go well with a black, white and grey-heavy color palette. Picking out certain materials can also spruce up a look, like picking out a leather item to add masculinity to a very feminine style. Casual clothes can also be dressed up with black heels or a long trench coat. Timeless pieces can be made trendier with the introduction of certain accessories or jewelry.

Even if your personal style falls on a broad category, it is always yours and yours alone. You mix it up with your choices and the way that you mix and match. More than the items in your closet and the price you pay for them, the thing that matters most is that you find comfort in what you wear. Your clothes should comfort you, bring out the best in you and make you feel like your best and most beautiful self. A closet filled with only your favorite and most loved items will bring peace and comfort to your daily life.

Thank You

As we reach the end of this book, I want to say thanks for reading this book.

I want to get this information out to as many people as possible. If you found this book helpful, I would greatly appreciate you leaving me a review. This helps others find the book as well.

Disclaimer

This document is geared towards providing exact and reliable information in regards to the topic and issue covered. The publication is sold on the idea that the publisher is not required to render an accounting, officially permitted, or otherwise, qualified services. If advice is necessary, legal, financial, medical or professional, a practiced individual in the profession should be ordered.

This information is not presented by a financial or medical practitioner and is for entertainment, educational and informational purposes only. The content is not intended as a substitute for professional medical advice, diagnosis, or treatment.

Always seek the advice of your physician or other qualified health care provider with any questions you may have regarding a medical condition. Never disregard professional medical advice or delay in seeking it because of something you have read.

The information provided herein is stated to be truthful and consistent, in that any liability, in terms of inattention or otherwise, by any usage or abuse of any policies, processes, or directions contained within is the solitary and utter re-

DISCLAIMER

sponsibility of the recipient reader.

Under no circumstances will any legal responsibility or blame be held against the publisher for any reparation, damages, or monetary loss due to the information herein, either directly or indirectly.

Last Updated: 14.Jun.2018

CPSIA information can be obtained
at www.ICGtesting.com
Printed in the USA
LVHW081035070223
738873LV00013B/500

9 788293 791041